Sleek SIAMESE

SOCIAL! SMART! VOCAL!

BLUE-EYED! LONG-LIVED!

ABDO
Publishing Company

Anders Hanson

Consulting Editor, Diane Craig, M.A./Reading Specialist

Published by ABDO Publishing Company
8000 West 78th Street, Edina, Minnesota 55439.

Copyright © 2010 by Abdo Consulting Group, Inc.
International copyrights reserved in all countries.

Printed in the United States.

 PRINTED ON RECYCLED PAPER

Editor: Liz Salzmann
Content Developer: Nancy Tuminelly
Cover and Interior Design and Production:
   Anders Hanson, Mighty Media
Illustrations: Bob Doucet
Photo Credits: Chanan (p.4–7), Karin Langner-Bahmann,
Shutterstock

Library of Congress Cataloging-in-Publication Data
Hanson, Anders, 1980-
  Sleek Siamese / Anders Hanson ; illustrations by Bob Doucet.
     p. cm. -- (Cat craze)
  ISBN 978-1-60453-725-3
  1. Siamese cat--Juvenile literature. I. Doucet, Bob, ill. II. Title.

SF449.S5H36 2010
636.8'25--dc22
                    2009011250

Super SandCastle™ books are created by a team of
professional educators, reading specialists, and content
developers around five essential components—phonemic
awareness, phonics, vocabulary, text comprehension, and
fluency—to assist young readers as they develop reading
skills and strategies and increase their general
knowledge. All books are written, reviewed, and leveled
for guided reading, early reading intervention, and
Accelerated Reader® programs for use in shared, guided,
and independent reading and writing activities to support
a balanced approach to literacy instruction.

CONTENTS

The Siamese	3
Facial Features	4
Body Basics	5
Coat & Color	6
Health & Care	8
Attitude & Behavior	10
Litters & Kittens	12
Buying a Siamese	14
Living with a Siamese	18
The Royal Siamese	20
Find the Siamese	22
The Siamese Quiz	23
Glossary	24

The
SIAMESE

The Siamese is one of the oldest cat **breeds**. Siamese cats come from Siam, which is now known as Thailand. In the Thai language, they are called *wichien-maat*, which means "moon diamond."

Siamese cats are friendly and social. They love to be around people.

FACIAL FEATURES

Head

Siamese cats have narrow, wedge-shaped heads.

Muzzle

A Siamese's **muzzle** is long and pointed.

Eyes

Siamese have blue, almond-shaped eyes. They are angled toward the nose.

Ears

Siamese have large, pointed ears.

There are two types of Siamese cat. The **modern Siamese** is described on these pages. The **traditional Siamese** looks different. Its body and face are more round. It has a shorter **muzzle** and smaller ears.

BODY BASICS

Size

Adult Siamese weigh 6 to 12 pounds (3 to 5 kg).

Build

Siamese cats have long, slender, muscular builds.

Tail

Siamese have long, thin tails. They are thicker at the base than at the tip.

Legs and Feet

Siamese have long legs. Their feet are small and oval.

COAT & COLOR

Siamese Fur

Siamese cats have short fur that lies close to their bodies. Their short coats draw attention to their lean, muscular bodies.

The Pointed Coat

A Siamese cat has light-colored fur on its body and neck. It has darker fur on its face, ears, legs, feet, and tail. These darker areas are called points. The points come in four colors. They are seal, chocolate, blue, and lilac.

Climate affects the coloring of pointed coats. Siamese cats that live where it's warm have lighter-colored coats. Siamese cats that live where it's cold have darker coats. Also, as a Siamese cat gets older, its entire coat darkens.

SEAL FUR

SEAL POINT

CHOCOLATE FUR

BLUE FUR

LILAC FUR

CHOCOLATE POINT

BLUE POINT

LILAC POINT

HEALTH & CARE

Life Span

Siamese cats can live a long time. Most Siamese live to be 15 to 20 years old.

Health Concerns

Siamese cats are generally quite healthy. In the past, many Siamese had crossed eyes and **kinked** tails. But **breeders** have been able to reduce those problems.

8

VET'S CHECKLIST

- Have your Siamese spayed or neutered. This will prevent unwanted kittens.

- Visit a vet for regular checkups.

- Clean your Siamese cat's teeth and ears once a week.

- Ask your vet about shots that may benefit your cat.

- Ask your vet which foods are right for your Siamese.

ATTITUDE & BEHAVIOR

Personality

Siamese cats are friendly. They love to be around people. Most Siamese like to sit on people's shoulders or curl up in their laps.

Siamese cats are more **vocal** than other cats. They often use their loud voices to demand attention. They can make loud noises that sound more like a crying baby than a cat.

Activity Level

Siamese cats are fairly active. They like to chase toys and climb furniture. But they enjoy quiet times of rest as well.

All About Me

Hi! My name is Sammy. I'm a Siamese. I just wanted to let you know a few things about me. I made some lists below of things I like and dislike. Check them out!

Things I Like

- Being around my family
- Using my voice to "talk" with my owner
- Playing with other Siamese
- Playing with toys
- Being petted

Things I Dislike

- Being left alone for a long time
- Not being included in my family's activities
- Being ignored when I am using my voice

LITTERS & KITTENS

Litter Size

Female Siamese usually give birth to four to six kittens.

Diet

Newborn kittens drink their mother's milk. They can begin to eat kitten food when they are about six weeks old. Kitten food is different from cat food. It has extra **protein**, fat, and **vitamins** that help kittens grow.

Color

All Siamese kittens are born pure white. Their colored points start to show when they are about one week old.

Growth

Siamese kittens should stay with their mothers for two to three months. A Siamese will be almost full grown when it is eight months old. But it will continue to grow slowly until it is one year old.

BUYING A SIAMESE

Choosing a Breeder

It's best to buy a kitten from a **breeder**, not a pet store. When you visit a cat breeder, ask to see the mother and father of the kittens. Make sure the parents are healthy, friendly, and well behaved.

Picking a Kitten

Choose a kitten that isn't too active or too shy. If you sit down, some of the kittens may come over to you. One of them might be the right one for you!

Is It the Right Cat for You?

Buying a cat is a big decision. You'll want to make sure your new pet suits your lifestyle.

Get out a piece of paper. Draw a line down the middle.

Read the statements listed here. Each time you agree with a statement from the left column, make a mark on the left side of your paper. When you agree with a statement from the right column, make a mark on the right side of your paper.

I want a social cat that needs a lot of attention.	☐ ☐	I want a cat that doesn't mind being left alone.
I like cats that "talk" a lot.	☐ ☐	I don't like noisy cats.
I want a cat that adores spending time with me.	☐ ☐	I want an independent cat.
I want a playful, friendly cat.	☐ ☐	I like lazy cats.
I like long, slender cats.	☐ ☐	I prefer heavy cats.

If you made more marks on the left side than on the right side, a Siamese may be the right cat for you! If you made more marks on the right side of your paper, you might want to consider another breed.

Some Things You'll Need

Cats go to the bathroom in a **litter box**. It should be kept in a quiet place. Most cats learn to use their litter box all by themselves. You just have to show them where it is! The dirty **litter** should be scooped out every day. The litter should be changed completely every week.

Your cat's **food and water dishes** should be wide and shallow. This helps your cat keep its whiskers clean. The dishes should be in a different area than the litter box. Cats do not like to eat and go to the bathroom in the same area.

Cats love to scratch! **Scratching posts** help keep cats from scratching the furniture. The scratching post should be taller than your cat. It should have a wide, heavy base so it won't tip over.

Cats are natural predators. Without small animals to hunt, cats may become bored and unhappy. **Cat toys** can satisfy your cat's need to chase and capture. They will help keep your cat entertained and happy.

Cats should not play with balls of yarn or string. If they accidentally eat the yarn, they could get sick.

Cat claws should be trimmed regularly with special cat claw **clippers**. Regular nail clippers will also work. Some people choose to have their cat's claws removed by a vet. But most vets and animal rights groups think declawing is cruel.

You should brush your cat regularly with a **cat hair brush**. This will help keep its coat healthy and clean.

A **cat bed** will give your cat a safe, comfortable place to sleep.

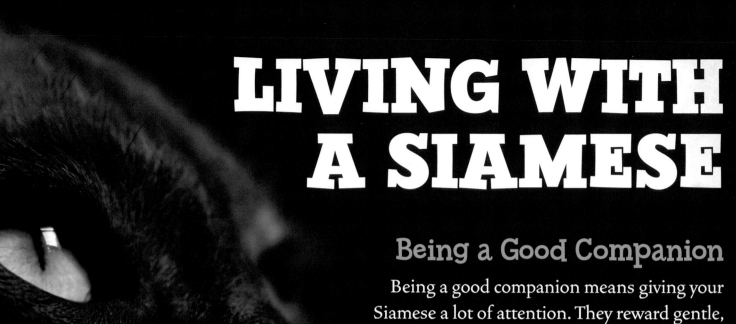

LIVING WITH A SIAMESE

Being a Good Companion

Being a good companion means giving your Siamese a lot of attention. They reward gentle, loving owners with life-long **devotion**.

Siamese cats are social. They don't like to be left alone for long periods. If your family is away from home during the day, consider getting two Siamese cats. They'll both be happy to have a playmate.

Inside or Outside?

Siamese cats can live inside or outside. But most vets say that it is best for them to be kept inside. That way they are safe from predators and cars.

Feeding Your Siamese

Feed your Siamese wet or dry cat food. Your vet can help you choose the best food for your cat.

Cleaning the Litter Box

Like all cats, Siamese are tidy. They don't like smelly or dirty litter boxes. If the litter box is dirty, they may go to the bathroom somewhere else. Ask your vet for advice if your cat isn't using its box.

☠ DANGER: POISONOUS FOODS

Some people like to feed their cats table scraps. Here are some human foods that can make cats sick.

TOMATOES

POTATOES

ONIONS

GARLIC

CHOCOLATE

GRAPES

THE ROYAL SIAMESE

Legend has it that Siamese cats were kept by royalty in Siam. The royal family of Siam believed in **reincarnation**. Whenever a royal person died, a Siamese cat from the palace was chosen to receive his or her soul.

The chosen cat was brought to a **Buddhist** temple. The temple monks treated the cat like royalty. They fed it the best foods on fancy gold plates. The cat's bed was made with the finest pillows. The lucky Siamese would spend the rest of its days living in luxury at the temple.

FIND THE SIAMESE

A

B

C

D

THE SIAMESE QUIZ

1. Siamese come from Siam, which is now known as Thailand. **True or false?**

2. Siamese cats have green eyes. **True or false?**

3. Siamese cats have pointed coats. **True or false?**

4. Siamese are vocal cats. **True or false?**

5. All Siamese kittens are born with dark coats. **True or false?**

6. Siamese like to be left alone for long periods. **True or false?**

Answers: 1) true 2) false 3) true 4) true 5) false 6) false

GLOSSARY

breed – a group of animals or plants with common ancestors. A *breeder* is someone whose job is to breed certain animals or plants.

Buddhist – one who believes in the teachings of Gautama Buddha.

devotion – a strong feeling of love and faith.

kink – a small, sharp bend.

legend – a story passed down through history that may not be true.

muzzle – an animal's nose and jaws.

protein – a substance found in all plant and animal cells.

reincarnation – the rebirth of a soul in a new body.

vitamin – a substance needed for good health, found naturally in plants and meats.

vocal – using the voice to make sounds or communicate.

About SUPER SANDCASTLE™

Bigger Books for Emerging Readers
Grades K–4

Created for library, classroom, and at-home use, Super SandCastle™ books support and engage young readers as they develop and build literacy skills and will increase their general knowledge about the world around them. Super SandCastle™ books are part of SandCastle™, the leading preK–3 imprint for emerging and beginning readers. Super SandCastle™ features a larger trim size for more reading fun.

Let Us Know

Super SandCastle™ would like to hear your stories about reading this book. What was your favorite page? Was there something hard that you needed help with? Share the ups and downs of learning to read. We want to hear from you! Send us an e-mail.

sandcastle@abdopublishing.com

Contact us for a complete list of SandCastle™, Super SandCastle™, and other nonfiction and fiction titles from ABDO Publishing Company.

www.abdopublishing.com • 8000 West 78th Street Edina, MN 55439 • 800-800-1312 • 952-831-1632 fax